K-2 READERS

HI! MAX AND ZOEY AGAIN.

YOU'VE PROBABLY HEARD THE WORD "BULLYING." BUT WHAT EXACTLY IS IT?

BULLYING IS WHEN SOMEONE IS MEAN TO ANOTHER PERSON AGAIN AND AGAIN.

IT IS ALSO WHEN ONE PERSON TURNS FRIENDS AGAINST ANOTHER PERSON.

SOME PEOPLE BULLY TO MAKE OTHERS LAUGH. IT MAKES THE PEOPLE WHO ARE BULLYING FEEL GOOD. OTHERS DO IT BECAUSE THEY ARE MAD AT THE PERSON THEY ARE BULLYING.

"BULLYING" IS NOT THE SAME AS "BOTHERING." BOTHERING IS WHEN SOMEONE IS BEING ANNOYING.

WHEN SOMEONE IS BEING ANNOYING, YOU CAN SIMPLY ASK THAT PERSON TO STOP.

BUT BULLYING IS WHEN SOMEONE BEING MEAN TO YOU MAKES YOU FEEL SAD, SCARED, OR LIKE THERE IS SOMETHING WRONG WITH YOU.

BULLYING IS ALSO WHEN YOU FEEL LOST AND ALONE BECAUSE SOMEONE MADE YOUR FRIENDS STOP LIKING YOU.

3

Learn to Apologize

7

REVIEW THE FOUR PARTS OF A GOOD APOLOGY:

1. SAY YOU ARE SORRY.

THIS LETS THE PERSON KNOW THAT YOU FEEL BADLY FOR WHAT YOU DID.

2. SAY WHAT YOU ARE SORRY FOR.

THIS LETS THE PERSON KNOW THAT YOU ACCEPT WHAT YOU DID AND THAT YOU BOTH AGREE ON WHAT YOU DID WRONG.

3. LET THE PERSON KNOW THAT HE OR SHE HAS A RIGHT TO BE MAD.

THIS LETS THE PERSON KNOW THAT IT'S OKAY TO GET MAD.

4. SAY YOU WILL NOT DO WHATEVER IT WAS YOU DID AGAIN.

THIS LETS THE PERSON KNOW THAT YOU REALLY MEAN IT.

ACTIVITY: PRACTICE!

YES, YOU CAN PRACTICE APOLOGIZING THE RIGHT WAY WITH A FRIEND. THINK OF SOMETHING THAT WOULD MAKE YOUR FRIEND ANGRY, LIKE TAKING A TOY OR A BOOK FROM YOUR FRIEND WITHOUT ASKING, THEN SAY THE FOUR-PART APOLOGY. AFTER YOU HAVE PRACTICED APOLOGIZING, HAVE YOUR FRIEND PRACTICE APOLOGIZING TO YOU.

Create a Circle of Friends

GIRLS, THIS SECTION IS FOR YOU. I'M GOING TO TELL YOU ABOUT HAVING A CIRCLE OF FRIENDS.

I KNOW IT'S GREAT TO HAVE A BEST FRIEND. YOU DO EVERYTHING TOGETHER AND TELL EACH OTHER SECRETS.

YOU THINK THAT ONE SPECIAL FRIEND IS ALL YOU NEED.

BUT THE TRUTH IS THAT FRIENDSHIPS CHANGE.

SOMETIMES OUR BEST FRIEND WANTS A NEW BEST FRIEND. AND THAT CAN REALLY HURT.

IT CAN LEAVE YOU FEELING LOST AND ALONE.

BUT THERE IS SOMETHING YOU CAN DO SO YOU ALWAYS HAVE A FRIEND.

The Strange Trouble with Three

NOW HERE IS SOMETHING THAT YOU MAY ALREADY KNOW ABOUT.

WE CALL IT THE "STRANGE TROUBLE WITH THREE."

DID YOU EVER NOTICE HOW WHEN YOU PLAY WITH ONE OTHER PERSON, IT CAN BE SO MUCH FUN...

...BUT WHEN ANOTHER PERSON JOINS YOU TO MAKE THREE, SOMETIMES ONE PERSON IS LEFT OUT?

THIS IS THE STRANGE TROUBLE WITH THREE. SOMETIMES WHEN THERE ARE THREE, ONE PERSON WILL BE LEFT OUT.

AND EVEN WORSE, SOMETIMES THE TWO WHO ARE PLAYING TOGETHER WILL START BEING MEAN TO THE THIRD PERSON.

Everyone Is Different

If Name-calling Makes You Upset

AT SOME POINT, EVERYONE GETS CALLED A NAME.

SOMETIMES THE NAME CAN BE FUNNY...

...BUT OTHER TIMES IT CAN HURT.

HEY, GOOFBALL!

HEY, UGLY!

WHEN SOMEONE CALLS YOU A NAME, YOU USUALLY THINK ABOUT HOW IT MAKES YOU FEEL INSTEAD OF WHAT THE PERSON IS SAYING.

BUT IF YOU STOP AND THINK ABOUT WHAT WORDS THE PERSON USES, YOU MAY NOT FEEL BADLY AT ALL.

FOR EXAMPLE, LET'S SAY SOMEONE CALLS YOU A "BABY."

ASK YOURSELF, ARE YOU REALLY A BABY?

BABY!

16

If You Are Being Bullied

18

19

20

21

Important Definitions

DON'T WORRY, THERE WON'T BE A QUIZ! BUT THESE WORDS WILL BE USED THROUGHOUT THE GUIDE, SO IT HELPS TO KNOW THEM.

WE DON'T CALL THE PERSON A "BULLY" SINCE THAT TERM IS A LABEL AND DOES NOT FULLY DESCRIBE THE PERSON.

AGGRESSOR:
Person who does the bullying.

"AGGRESSOR" IS USED BECAUSE THE PERSON DOING THE BULLYING IS USING "AGGRESSIVE" BEHAVIOR. AGGRESSIVE BEHAVIOR IS ANOTHER WAY OF SAYING "BULLYING" BEHAVIOR. AGGRESSIVE BEHAVIOR INCLUDES PUSHING, THREATS, INSULTS, MOCKING, AND HARMING A PERSON'S FRIENDSHIPS.

A **TARGET** IS THE PERSON WHO IS HARMED BY THE BULLYING BEHAVIOR.

TARGET:
Person who is being bullied.

ANYONE CAN BE A **TARGET** OF BULLYING BEHAVIOR, SO A MORE ACCURATE TERM FOR A PERSON HARMED BY BULLYING IS "HARMED TARGET." BUT TO KEEP THINGS SIMPLE, FOR THE REST OF THE GUIDE, WE'LL SIMPLY CALL A PERSON HARMED BY BULLYING A "TARGET."

THERE ARE THREE TYPES OF BULLYING: PHYSICAL, VERBAL, AND FRIENDSHIP HARMING.

THE TYPE OF BULLYING DESCRIBES THE AGGRESSION THAT IS USED. REMEMBER, "AGGRESSION" IS JUST A WORD THAT MEANS "BULLYING BEHAVIOR."

Physical bullying – pushing, shoving, standing in an intimidating way, making threatening gestures, or verbally threatening to harm the target. This type of bullying is meant to make the target fear being harmed and to feel scared. The aggressor does this to try to get respect from anyone watching.

THE PURPOSE OF PHYSICAL BULLYING IS TO SHOW OTHERS THAT THE AGGRESSOR SHOULD BE FEARED, WHICH CAN EARN THE AGGRESSOR RESPECT.

BOTH BOYS AND GIRLS BULLY IN THIS WAY.

THAT'S TRUE.

Verbal bullying – commenting on, teasing, mocking, or insulting some aspect of the target, such as a part of his or her body, way of dressing, or where the target is from. This type of bullying makes the target feel flawed and like he or she is not the same as his or her classmates. The aggressor does this to become more popular.

THE PURPOSE OF VERBAL BULLYING IS TO GET OTHERS TO LAUGH AT SOME ASPECT OR CHARACTERISTIC OF THE TARGET.

THIS CAN MAKE THE AGGRESSOR APPEAR FUNNY AND CLEVER.

BOTH BOYS AND GIRLS BULLY IN THIS WAY.

Friendship harming – actions that make others not want to be friends with the target. These actions can include starting rumors and petitions, gossiping, and excluding. This type of bullying leaves the target feeling sad and alone. The aggressor does this to preserve her own popularity or to get back at the target for something the target did that made the aggressor upset.

WHILE BOTH BOYS AND GIRLS CAN HARM THE FRIENDSHIPS OF OTHERS, FRIENDSHIP HARMING IS A TYPE OF BULLYING MOST COMMONLY USED BY GIRLS.

Why Do People Bully?

How People Bully and the **TOP SECRET FACTS** They Don't Want You to Know

KNOWING HOW BULLYING WORKS IS IMPORTANT, AS IT THEN ALLOWS INTENDED TARGETS TO PREVENT IT FROM HAPPENING IN THE FIRST PLACE AND TO STOP IT FROM HAPPENING IF IT IS IN PROGRESS.

REMEMBER, THERE ARE THREE WAYS THAT PEOPLE BULLY: PHYSICAL (INTIMIDATION), VERBAL (INSULTS AND MOCKING), AND FRIENDSHIP HARMING.

PHYSICAL (INTIMIDATION)

AGGRESSORS SCARE TARGETS BY MAKING THEM THINK THEY WILL BE PHYSICALLY HARMED.

THE AGGRESSOR CAN MAKE THREATS...

...STAND IN AN INTIMIDATING WAY...

...GIVE MEAN LOOKS...

...AND PUSH AND SHOVE THE TARGET.

THIS IS TYPICAL OF HOW BOYS BULLY.

GIRLS ALSO BULLY IN THIS WAY.

BUT HERE'S THE SECRET:

29

30

Find Your Section

NOW THAT YOU KNOW THE BASICS, FIND YOUR SECTION:

TO HELP SOMEONE WHO IS BEING BULLIED, *GO TO PAGE 32.*

TO LEARN WAYS OF RESPONDING TO BULLYING BEHAVIOR SO THAT YOU AREN'T BULLIED, *GO TO PAGE 42.*

TO STOP SOMEONE FROM BULLYING YOU, *GO TO PAGE 68.*

TARGET

TO TEACH AN ADULT HOW TO HELP YOU, *GO TO PAGE 76.*

HOW TO HELP A BULLIED PERSON

THE GOOD NEWS IS THAT THERE IS A LOT YOU CAN DO TO HELP.

BUT THERE ARE SOME THINGS YOU NEED TO KNOW.

DOING SOMETHING ABOUT BULLYING ISN'T EASY.

YOU MAY BE AFRAID THE AGGRESSOR WILL START BULLYING YOU.

YIKES!

AND DOING SOMETHING CAN FEEL LIKE YOU ARE CHOOSING SIDES AGAINST SOMEONE WHO MAY BE MORE POPULAR THAN THE PERSON YOU ARE TRYING TO HELP.

YOU MAY WORRY THAT YOU ARE RISKING YOUR OWN FRIENDSHIPS JUST TO HELP SOMEONE WHO MAY NOT REALLY BE YOUR FRIEND.

How to Help Indirectly

BUT THERE ARE MANY WAYS TO HELP STOP BULLYING WITHOUT FEAR OF BEING BULLIED OR FEELING LIKE YOU HAVE TO CHOOSE SIDES. THESE ACTIONS ARE CALLED "HELPING INDIRECTLY."

REFUSE TO JOIN IN THE BULLYING

DON'T LAUGH, MAKE ADDITIONAL COMMENTS, OR EVEN STAND LIKE YOU'RE ON THE SIDE OF THE AGGRESSOR. DON'T JOIN IN.

DON'T REWARD THE AGGRESSOR

DON'T SHOW ADMIRATION FOR THE AGGRESSOR OR APPROVAL OF THE BULLYING.

IN PRIVATE, SUPPORT THE TARGET

LET THE TARGET KNOW THAT YOU DON'T LIKE THE BULLYING EITHER. YOU CAN ALSO SUGGEST THAT THE TARGET GET HELP, EITHER FROM THIS GUIDE OR FROM AN ADULT.

THAT GUY WAS A REAL JERK.

Helping to Stop
PHYSICAL AND VERBAL BULLYING

IF YOU SEE PHYSICAL OR VERBAL BULLYING HAPPENING...

...TO EITHER A BOY OR A GIRL...

...YOU CAN TRY TELLING THE AGGRESSOR TO STOP. OR YOU CAN DISRUPT THE BULLYING BY PRETENDING TO BE UNAWARE OR NOT TO CARE. HERE ARE SOME EXAMPLES. YOU CAN SAY WHAT YOU THINK IS BEST.

PRETEND TO BE UNAWARE: DISRUPT THE BULLYING

HEY GUYS, WHAT'S GOING ON?

PRETEND TO BE UNAWARE: DIVERT ATTENTION

DO YOU GUYS WANT TO KICK A BALL AROUND?

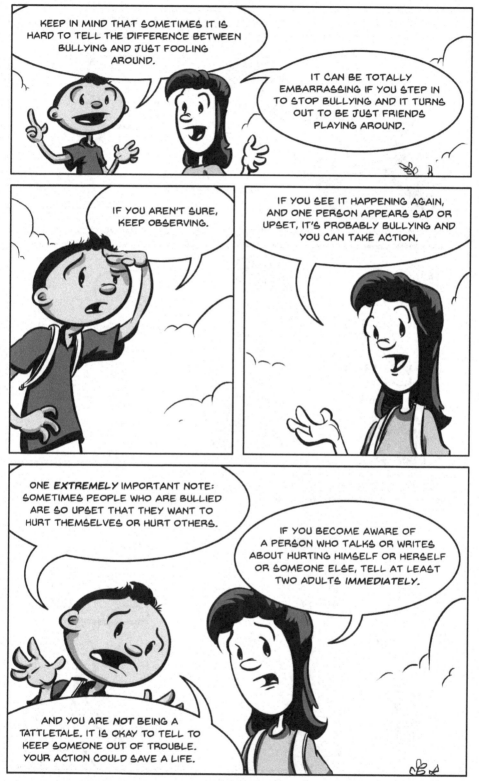

KEEP IN MIND THAT SOMETIMES IT IS HARD TO TELL THE DIFFERENCE BETWEEN BULLYING AND JUST FOOLING AROUND.

IT CAN BE TOTALLY EMBARRASSING IF YOU STEP IN TO STOP BULLYING AND IT TURNS OUT TO BE JUST FRIENDS PLAYING AROUND.

IF YOU AREN'T SURE, KEEP OBSERVING.

IF YOU SEE IT HAPPENING AGAIN, AND ONE PERSON APPEARS SAD OR UPSET, IT'S PROBABLY BULLYING AND YOU CAN TAKE ACTION.

ONE *EXTREMELY* IMPORTANT NOTE: SOMETIMES PEOPLE WHO ARE BULLIED ARE SO UPSET THAT THEY WANT TO HURT THEMSELVES OR HURT OTHERS.

IF YOU BECOME AWARE OF A PERSON WHO TALKS OR WRITES ABOUT HURTING HIMSELF OR HERSELF OR SOMEONE ELSE, TELL AT LEAST TWO ADULTS *IMMEDIATELY.*

AND YOU ARE *NOT* BEING A TATTLETALE. IT IS OKAY TO TELL TO KEEP SOMEONE OUT OF TROUBLE. YOUR ACTION COULD SAVE A LIFE.

BULLYPROOF YOURSELF:
How to Keep Others from Bullying You

LET'S TALK ABOUT HOW YOU CAN STOP SOMEONE FROM BULLYING YOU. WE CALL IT THE DIFFERENCE BETWEEN "REACTING" AND "RESPONDING."

IT IS NORMAL TO "REACT" TO PHYSICAL AND VERBAL BULLYING BY SHOWING FEAR OR GETTING UPSET.

BUT REACTING IN THOSE WAYS IS WHAT CAN MAKE BULLYING SUCCESSFUL. YOU MUST "RESPOND" IN A WAY THAT MAKES IT FAIL.

PHYSICAL BULLYING FAILS WHEN YOU RESPOND BY APPEARING UNAFRAID, BECAUSE THE AGGRESSOR ONLY GETS RESPECT FROM THOSE WATCHING WHEN YOU ARE AFRAID. VERBAL BULLYING IS MUCH MORE EFFECTIVE FOR THE AGGRESSOR WHEN YOU REACT BY GETTING UPSET. AN AGGRESSOR GAINS POPULARITY WHEN OTHERS LAUGH, AND GETTING UPSET ENSURES THAT OTHERS WILL LAUGH. BUT IF YOU RESPOND IN A DIFFERENT WAY, LIKE BY APPEARING UNAFFECTED, OTHERS MAY NOT LAUGH, AND THE AGGRESSOR WILL NOT GAIN ANYTHING.

SUCCEEDS: YOU REACT BY SHOWING FEAR OR GETTING UPSET AND EVERYONE CAN SEE IT. AGGRESSOR GETS A STATUS BOOST!

FAILS: YOU RESPOND BY NOT GETTING UPSET OR SCARED. AGGRESSOR GETS NO BOOST!

FRIENDSHIP HARMING...

...ALSO KNOWN AS "GIRL BULLYING"...

...IS DIFFERENT. IT IS OFTEN "COVERT," WHICH MEANS HAPPENS IN SECRET. SO YOU DON'T KNOW IT IS HAPPENING UNTIL DAMAGE HAS BEEN DONE. BECAUSE OF THAT, THE BEST WAY TO DEAL WITH IT IS TO PREVENT IT FROM HAPPENING. BUT IF IT DOES START, THERE ARE THINGS YOU CAN DO TO STOP IT.

44

INTIMIDATION

SUCCEEDS: REACT BY COWERING, SHRINKING BACK, SHOWING FEAR, OR TRYING TO GET AWAY.

FAILS: RESPOND BY SHOWING NO FEAR, STANDING TALL, WALKING WITH CONFIDENCE, AND LOOKING THE AGGRESSOR IN THE EYE.

REMEMBER, AGGRESSORS RARELY INTEND PHYSICAL HARM. THEY JUST WANT TO SCARE YOU SO THAT ANYONE WATCHING THINKS THE AGGRESSOR IS SOMEONE TO BE FEARED.

MEAN REMARK

SUCCEEDS: REACT BY GETTING MAD, SAD, OR FRUSTRATED, OR MAKING A MEAN REMARK BACK.

FAILS: RESPOND BY PRETENDING NOT TO BE BOTHERED OR DOING SOMETHING UNEXPECTED, LIKE LAUGHING AT THE REMARK OR AGREEING WITH THE AGGRESSOR.

PLEASE NOTE THAT PRETENDING NOT TO BE BOTHERED IS NOT THE SAME THING AS IGNORING A REMARK. LET THE AGGRESSOR AND ANYONE WATCHING KNOW YOU HEARD IT SO THAT YOU CAN RESPOND BY SHOWING YOU AREN'T BOTHERED.

SAYING A CHARACTERISTIC IS A FLAW

NICE DRESS!

NICE DRESS!

THANKS!

SUCCEEDS: REACT BY GETTING UPSET AND FEELING FLAWED OR LIKE YOU NEED TO CHANGE.

FAILS: RESPOND BY SHOWING PRIDE IN WHO YOU ARE, HOW YOU DRESS, AND HOW YOU LOOK.

DON'T FORGET, EVERYONE IS *UNIQUE* AND DIFFERENT IN SOME WAY.

THE AGGRESSOR JUST WANTS THOSE WATCHING TO LAUGH OR THINK THAT HE OR SHE IS REALLY CLEVER.

GETTING UPSET WILL JUST MAKE EVERYONE WATCHING LAUGH HARDER. IF YOU RESPOND BY NOT GETTING UPSET, THE BULLYING IS NOT AS FUNNY AND MAY FAIL.

AND YOU CAN'T SIMPLY IGNORE BULLYING BEHAVIOR. AN AGGRESSOR WILL KNOW HE OR SHE IS UPSETTING YOU IF YOU JUST TRY TO PRETEND IT ISN'T HAPPENING AND HOPE IT WILL STOP. YOU HAVE TO ACTIVELY RESPOND TO THE BULLYING IN SOME WAY TO SHOW THAT YOU ARE *NOT* UPSET.

ALSO, THESE WAYS OF RESPONDING TO BULLYING TO GET IT TO STOP CAN TAKE TIME BECAUSE YOU AREN'T SIMPLY ACTING DIFFERENTLY - YOU HAVE TO CONVINCE THE AGGRESSOR THAT YOU ARE NO LONGER UPSET. IF IT DOESN'T WORK THE FIRST TIME, *KEEP TRYING!*

How to make
~~FRIENDSHIP HARMING~~ FAIL
GIRL BULLYING

GIRLS, THIS SECTION IS FOR YOU. I'M GOING TO TELL YOU ABOUT WAYS YOU CAN PREVENT FRIENDSHIP HARMING FROM STARTING AND HOW TO STOP IT WHEN IT DOES.

GIRLS, I KNOW I'M GENERALIZING, BUT WE USUALLY DON'T TELL OUR FRIENDS WHEN OR WHY WE ARE ANGRY, AND WE VALUE OUR FRIENDS ABOVE **ALL ELSE** (WHICH IS WHY WE KEEP OUR ANGER TO OURSELVES). WE OFTEN TAKE ACTIONS THAT HARM FRIENDSHIPS INSTEAD OF TELLING SOMEONE THAT WE ARE ANGRY. FRIENDSHIP HARMING AVOIDS CONFRONTATION, AND WE THINK IT WILL ALLOW US TO PRESERVE THE FRIENDSHIP WHILE GETTING JUSTICE FOR THE OFFENSE.

CLAP

BUT FRIENDSHIP HARMING DOESN'T RESOLVE THE CONFLICT. WE CAN HURT OUR FRIENDS MORE THAN WE INTEND, AND FRIENDS CAN DO THE SAME TO US, CREATING A HUGE MESS. **EXPRESSING** ANGER, **OWNING UP** TO OUR ACTIONS, AND **APOLOGIZING** THE RIGHT WAY ARE THE KEYS TO PREVENTING AND STOPPING FRIENDSHIP HARMING.

OF COURSE, SOME FRIENDSHIP HARMING DOES NOT **START** FROM CONFLICT. IT CAN ARISE FROM JEALOUSY, FROM WANTING TO BE MORE POPULAR, TO STRENGTHEN FRIENDSHIPS IN A GROUP BY TARGETING ONE MEMBER, AND SIMPLY BECAUSE SOME GIRLS FEEL GOOD WHEN DOING IT. IN THESE CASES, TALKING TO AGGRESSORS **DIRECTLY** SO THEY GET TO KNOW YOU AND HAVING A LARGE CIRCLE OF FRIENDS WHO CAN STAND BY YOU CAN HELP.

ACCEPT AN APOLOGY AND MOVE ON

YOUR FRIEND SAID SOMETHING EMBARRASSING ABOUT YOU TO YOUR OTHER FRIENDS. SHE REALIZES THAT SHE HURT YOU AND SHE'S SORRY. SHE APOLOGIZES.

I'M SORRY FOR...

58

NEVER POST ONLINE, EMAIL, OR TEXT WHEN ANGRY

YOU GET AN EMAIL WITH A MEAN REMARK ABOUT YOUR HAIR FROM ONE OF YOUR FRIENDS. SHE HAS COPIED WHAT SEEMS LIKE HALF THE CLASS. YOU ARE FURIOUS.

OPTION 1: REACT

YOU "REPLY ALL" WITH A MEAN COMMENT ABOUT YOUR FRIEND. NOW YOU ARE BOTH ANGRY. FRIENDS START TO TAKE SIDES. A "WAR" HAS BEGUN.

OPTION 2: TALK DIRECTLY

YOU WAIT UNTIL YOU FEEL CALM AND THEN TALK DIRECTLY TO YOUR FRIEND. SHE APOLOGIZES AND EVEN AGREES TO SEND ANOTHER EMAIL TO EVERYONE WITH HER APOLOGY. YOU ACCEPT THE APOLOGY AND MOVE ON.

62

64

65

STOP BULLYING THAT IS HAPPENING TO YOU

YOU'RE BEING BULLIED. IT'S HARD TO ADMIT, EVEN TO YOURSELF. YOU MAY FEEL LIKE THERE IS SOMETHING WRONG WITH YOU OR THAT THE BULLYING IS YOUR FAULT. YOU MAY FEEL LIKE YOU ARE WEAK OR UNPOPULAR. YOU MAY HAVE LOST YOUR FRIENDS, OR FRIENDS MAY NOW BE EXCLUDING YOU, AND YOU HAVE NO IDEA WHY. YOU MAY FEEL LOST, ALONE, OR SCARED. WHAT SHOULD YOU DO?

FIRST, YOU NEED TO REALIZE THAT **THE BULLYING IS NOT YOUR FAULT.** NO MATTER WHO YOU ARE, WHERE YOU ARE FROM, WHAT YOU LOOK LIKE, OR WHAT YOU BELIEVE IN, NO ONE DESERVES TO BE BULLIED. YOU ARE BEING BULLIED BECAUSE SOMEONE OR A GROUP OF PEOPLE ARE TRYING TO BE MORE POPULAR OR RESPECTED AND ARE USING YOU TO DO IT.

SECOND, YOU NEED TO BELIEVE THAT **YOU ARE NOT FLAWED.** ANY PART OF YOU THAT THE AGGRESSOR IS MOCKING OR INSULTING IS JUST AN EXCUSE TO BULLY YOU. EVERYBODY IS UNIQUE IN SOME WAY, EVEN AGGRESSORS. AND BEING BULLIED DOESN'T MEAN YOU ARE WEAK. SO YOU MUST UNDERSTAND AND BELIEVE THAT. YOU DO FIT IN WITH YOUR FRIENDS AND CLASSMATES. YOU DO BELONG.

FOURTH, YOU NEED TO **DECIDE IF YOU WANT AN ADULT HELPER.** YES, WE KNOW – AN ADULT MAY BE THE LAST PERSON YOU MAY WANT TO TALK TO. NOT ONLY IS IT HARD TO ADMIT TO BEING BULLIED, BUT YOU'RE ALSO WORRIED THE ADULT MIGHT MAKE THINGS WORSE. YOU CERTAINLY DON'T WANT THE AGGRESSOR TO KNOW YOU'VE TOLD OR TO GET IN TROUBLE AND THEN TAKE IT OUT ON YOU. AND MOST IMPORTANTLY, YOU WANT TO SOLVE THIS PROBLEM YOURSELF.

BUT WOULDN'T IT BE GOOD TO HAVE SOMEONE TO TALK TO WHEN YOU ARE FEELING SCARED AND ALONE? WOULDN'T IT BE GREAT TO TALK ABOUT THE DIFFERENT RESPONSES YOU ARE TRYING OUT AND REPORT BACK ON HOW THEY ARE WORKING? WOULDN'T IT BE HELPFUL TO TALK TO SOMEONE WHO HAS ALREADY FACED AND GONE THROUGH THE SAME THINGS THAT YOU ARE FACING NOW?

GETTING ADULT HELP DOES **NOT** MEAN THE ADULT IS GOING TO TALK TO THE AGGRESSOR, GET THE AGGRESSOR IN TROUBLE, OR MAKE THINGS WORSE. THE FACT IS, ADULTS CAN BE A **HUGE** HELP, IF THEY HELP IN THE RIGHT WAY. ADULTS WHO HELP IN THE RIGHT WAY WILL TAKE YOUR PROBLEM SERIOUSLY. THEY WILL LISTEN AND UNDERSTAND WHAT YOU ARE GOING THROUGH. AND THEY WILL WORK WITH YOU TO CREATE A PLAN TO SOLVE THE PROBLEM.

THE IMPORTANT THING IS THAT ALTHOUGH YOUR HELPER IS AN ADULT, THE PLAN THAT YOU CREATE TO STOP THE BULLYING IS ONE THAT YOU DEVELOP TOGETHER.

YOU HAVE A SAY IN WHAT HAPPENS.

YOU AND YOUR ADULT HELPER DECIDE TOGETHER WHAT TO DO NEXT.

IF THERE IS AN ADULT YOU FEEL YOU CAN TRUST BUT ARE NOT SURE IF HE OR SHE WILL HELP IN THE RIGHT WAY, YOU CAN ACTUALLY **TRAIN THE ADULT** ON HOW TO HELP YOU. THE NEXT SECTION OF THIS GUIDE, **"TRAIN YOUR ADULT HELPER,"** CAN SHOW AN ADULT EXACTLY HOW TO HELP. READ THAT SECTION WITH THE ADULT THAT YOU TRUST. THEN ASK THE ADULT HOW HE OR SHE WOULD HELP A PERSON BEING BULLIED. WOULD THE ADULT TAKE ACTION WITHOUT TALKING TO YOU FIRST? OR WOULD THE ADULT HELP YOU CREATE A PLAN THAT YOU EXECUTE TOGETHER?

IF YOU FEEL COMFORTABLE WITH THE ANSWERS, YOU HAVE FOUND YOUR ADULT HELPER. IF NOT, YOU SHOULD FIND ANOTHER ADULT. AND IF YOU GOT THIS GUIDE FROM YOUR SCHOOL, THE TEACHERS AND ADMINISTRATORS MAY HAVE ALREADY BEEN TRAINED ON HOW TO PROVIDE HELP THE RIGHT WAY.

A PLAN TO STOP BULLYING CAN BE SIMPLE. FIRST, YOU CAN BOTH READ THE SECTION **"BULLYING BASICS"** AND THEN DISCUSS HOW YOU ARE BEING BULLIED. HAVING SOMEONE TO DISCUSS IT WITH CAN HELP YOU SEE YOUR BULLYING PROBLEM DIFFERENTLY, MORE CLEARLY. SECOND, YOU CAN SAY YOU KNOW THAT THE BULLYING IS NOT YOUR FAULT AND YOU ARE NOT FLAWED. THEN YOU CAN DECIDE WHAT YOUR NEXT ACTION WILL BE. DO YOU WANT TO TRY TO STOP IT YOURSELF USING THE RESPONSES THAT CAN MAKE AGGRESSION FAIL? IF SO, READ THE SECTION **"BULLYPROOF YOURSELF"** WITH THE ADULT AND CHOOSE RESPONSES THAT MAKE SENSE FOR YOUR BULLYING SITUATION.

THE ADULT ALSO MIGHT HAVE SOME GOOD SUGGESTIONS, SUCH AS GETTING INVOLVED IN ACTIVITIES WHERE YOU CAN MAKE NEW FRIENDS. OR PERHAPS YOU'D LIKE THE ADULT TO HAVE A CONVERSATION WITH THE AGGRESSOR TO ASK THE AGGRESSOR TO STOP. THIS DOES **NOT** MEAN THE AGGRESSOR WILL GET IN TROUBLE. IT WOULD JUST BE A FRIENDLY CHAT TO ASK THE AGGRESSOR TO STOP. OR THE BULLYING MIGHT BE GETTING TO BE TOO MUCH, MORE THAN YOU CAN HANDLE, AND YOU MIGHT WANT THE ADULT TO MAKE THE BULLYING STOP. IT'S UP TO YOU. IT'S A PLAN YOU'VE HELPED CREATE.

REMEMBER, EVERY GREAT SPORTS PLAYER HAS A COACH, SOMEONE TO HELP AND GUIDE. GETTING HELP FROM AN ADULT IS LIKE GETTING A COACH. A COACH CAN GUIDE YOU, TALK THROUGH YOUR NEXT MOVES, AND HELP FIGURE OUT THE BEST PLAYS FOR YOU TO MAKE TO GET THE BULLYING TO STOP.
AND YOU CAN GET THE BULLYING TO STOP. IT MIGHT SEEM LIKE A HARD THING TO DO, BUT ONCE YOU TRY, YOU MIGHT BE SURPRISED AT HOW EASY IT IS.

TRAIN YOUR ADULT HELPER

SIT, DAD! NOW ROLL OVER!

GETTING ADULT HELP CAN BE ONE OF THE MOST EFFECTIVE WAYS TO GET BULLYING TO STOP.

IF THE BULLYING GETS REALLY BAD, IT'S BEST TO HAVE AN ADULT ON YOUR SIDE.

PARENTS AND TEACHERS WANT TO STOP BULLYING. BUT SOMETIMES THEY AREN'T AWARE IT IS HAPPENING, EVEN IF THEY SEE THE BULLYING BEHAVIOR. YOU NEED TO TELL THEM!

TALKING WITH AN ADULT CAN MAKE YOU FEEL BETTER, YOU CAN BOTH TALK ABOUT WHAT TO DO, AND THE ADULT CAN TAKE ACTION IF NECESSARY.

HOWEVER, YOU MAY ACTUALLY NEED TO TRAIN YOUR ADULT HELPER! SOME ADULTS HAVE NO IDEA WHAT TO DO, AND THEY MAY GIVE YOU BAD ADVICE.

BUT IT DOESN'T MEAN THE ADULTS DON'T CARE OR THAT YOUR PROBLEM IS NOT IMPORTANT!

YOU CAN TRAIN AN ADULT HELPER YOURSELF. JUST READ THE NEXT SECTION TOGETHER.

OKAY, DAD, NOW SHAKE!

HEY, ADULT!

IF A YOUNG PERSON HAS JUST PRESENTED YOU WITH THIS BOOK, THIS PERSON HAS A PROBLEM AND NEEDS YOUR HELP. PLEASE PLEASE PLEASE SIT WITH THIS PERSON AND READ THIS SECTION. THIS PERSON NEEDS YOUR SUPPORT, AND THE NEXT FEW PAGES WILL TELL YOU HOW YOU CAN DO IT. ARE YOU SITTING WITH THE PERSON IN A QUIET ROOM WITH NO DISTRACTIONS?

IF SO, PLEASE CONTINUE READING.

80

81

BORING ADULT STUFF

WHAT *YOU* CAN DO ABOUT BULLYING BY MAX AND ZOEY

CONCEPT AND TEXT BY ARI MAGNUSSON
ART AND LAYOUT BY GREG MARATHAS

ACKNOWLEDGMENTS

A HUGE THANKS TO **MICHELE DAVIS**, PRINCIPAL OF THE WARREN PRESCOTT K-8 SCHOOL, BOSTON PUBLIC SCHOOLS, AND **DR. DOMENIC AMARA**, FORMER ACADEMIC SUPERINTENDENT FOR MIDDLE AND K-8 SCHOOLS, BOSTON PUBLIC SCHOOLS, FOR PROVIDING THE IMPETUS TO CREATE THE *CIRCLEPOINT BULLYING PREVENTION PROGRAM*, OF WHICH THIS COMIC IS A COMPONENT; **KAREN ELIAS**, KINDERGARTEN TEACHER, BOSTON PUBLIC SCHOOLS, FOR HER INVALUABLE FEEDBACK AND INSIGHTS; AND THE **TEACHERS**, **PARENTS**, AND **STUDENTS** OF THE WARREN PRESCOTT K-8 SCHOOL IN CHARLESTOWN, MASSACHUSETTS, FOR THEIR SUPPORT IN PILOTING THIS COMIC.

A SPECIAL THANKS TO **ISRAEL C. KALMAN, MS**, A NOTED SCHOOL PSYCHOLOGIST, PSYCHOTHERAPIST, LECTURER, AUTHOR, BULLYING EXPERT, AND REVIEWER AND CRITIC OF BULLYING PREVENTION PROGRAMS, FOR HIS EARLY GUIDANCE ON VARIOUS BULLYING CONCEPTS. MANY OF THE PHYSICAL AND VERBAL BULLYING EMPOWERMENT TECHNIQUES IN THIS GUIDE ARE BASED ON THOSE CONTAINED IN HIS EXCELLENT BOOKS *BULLIES TO BUDDIES: HOW TO TURN YOUR ENEMIES INTO FRIENDS* AND *SUPER-DREN, THE DE-VICTIMIZER*.

AND AN EXTRA THANKS TO **DEREK MILLER** OF WESTWOOD, MA, FOR HIS VALUABLE FEEDBACK AND CONTINUED SUPPORT.

ABOUT THE AUTHOR

ARI MAGNUSSON IS A BULLYING PREVENTION RESEARCHER AND WRITER AND THE CREATOR OF THE *CIRCLEPOINT BULLYING PREVENTION PROGRAM*. HE IS THE BULLYING PREVENTION EDUCATOR FOR THE MASSACHUSETTS GENERAL HOSPITAL'S LIFE SKILLS AFTER-SCHOOL PROGRAM, OFFERED IN BOSTON-AREA SCHOOLS. HIS OTHER WRITINGS INCLUDE *ALL ABOUT BULLYING*, A BULLYING PREVENTION GUIDE FOR STUDENTS IN GRADES SIX AND UP; *BITOPIA*, A MIDDLE GRADE NOVEL ABOUT BULLIED CHILDREN THAT WAS NAMED ONE OF THE BEST BOOKS OF THE YEAR BY *KIRKUS REVIEWS*, AND NUMEROUS BLOGS AND ARTICLES.

ABOUT THE ILLUSTRATOR

GREG MARATHAS BEGAN HIS LIFE AS AN ARTIST ON HIS GRANDMOTHER'S FLOOR AT THE AGE OF SIX, CURLED UP WITH A PEN, PAPER, AND ART INSTRUCTION BOOKS. A LIFELONG CRAYOLA ADDICT, HE HAS SINCE BRANCHED OUT INTO VARIOUS DIGITAL AND TRADITIONAL ART-MAKING TECHNIQUES, THOUGH PENCILS AND CRAYONS WILL ALWAYS RETAIN A SPECIAL PLACE IN HIS HEART. HE RECEIVED HIS BFA IN ILLUSTRATION FROM LESLEY UNIVERSITY COLLEGE OF ART AND DESIGN.

LEGAL MUMBO JUMBO SECTION

ALL NAMES, PEOPLE, AND PLACES MENTIONED, DESCRIBED, AND DEPICTED IN THIS BOOK ARE FICTIONAL. ANY RESEMBLANCE TO ACTUAL NAMES, PEOPLE, AND PLACES IS ENTIRELY COINCIDENTAL.

COPYRIGHT © 2017 BY ARI MAGNUSSON
ALL RIGHTS RESERVED.

PUBLISHED BY
OLIVANDER PRESS LLC
BOSTON, MASSACHUSETTS
OLIVANDER, OLIVANDER PRESS, CIRCLEPOINT,
CIRCLEPOINT BULLYING PREVENTION PROGRAM,
AND ASSOCIATED LOGOS ARE TRADEMARKS OF OLIVANDER PRESS LLC.

NO PART OF THIS BOOK MAY BE REPRODUCED IN ANY FORM BY ANY MEANS WITHOUT WRITTEN PERMISSION OF THE PUBLISHER. PERMISSION IS NEVER GRANTED FOR COMMERCIAL PURPOSES. FOR INFORMATION OR TO MAKE A REQUEST REGARDING PERMISSIONS, PLEASE CONTACT OLIVANDER PRESS VIA THE CIRCLEPOINT PROGRAM WEBSITE, WWW.CIRCLEPOINTPROGRAM.ORG.

PAPERBACK ISBN-13: 978-0-9970221-8-6
EBOOK ISBN-13: 978-0-9970221-9-3

SECOND EDITION — JULY 2017

PRINTED IN THE UNITED STATES OF AMERICA

COVER AND ALL IMAGES COPYRIGHT © 2017 BY ARI MAGNUSSON

MORE INFORMATION

THIS COMIC IS A COMPONENT OF THE CIRCLEPOINT BULLYING PREVENTION PROGRAM, A COMPREHENSIVE PROGRAM FOR SCHOOLS AND ORGANIZATIONS THAT EMPOWERS ALL COMMUNITY MEMBERS WITH ROLE-APPROPRIATE ACTIONS AND STRATEGIES TO PREVENT, REDUCE, AND STOP BULLYING THAT WORK AT THE INDIVIDUAL, PEER GROUP, ORGANIZATION, AND COMMUNITY LEVELS. FOR MORE INFORMATION ON THE PROGRAM AND MATERIALS, INCLUDING A FREE BULLYING PREVENTION GUIDE FOR PARENTS, PLEASE VISIT THE CIRCLEPOINT PROGRAM WEBSITE.

WWW.CIRCLEPOINTPROGRAM.ORG

Made in USA - Kendallville, IN
86266_9780997022186
08 31 2022 1327